AS-SAUM (FASTING)

A BRIEF INTRODUCTION IN THE LIGHT OF QURAN & SAHIH HADITH

DR. FASIL BARKAT

ISBN 979-8886293227-7

THIS BOOK IS DEDICATED TO MY BELOVED
GRANDMOTHER

LATE MRS. ZAINUB BEGUM

Contents

Foreword

Indeed, all praise is for Allah and blessings of Allah be upon our beloved Prophetﷺ, Hisﷺ family, and Hisﷺ Companions. The main source of Islamic Sharee'ah is the Quran, it covers the divine orders, guiding principles and other facts in a general form. The second source is the Prophetic Hadith that are the traditions of the Prophetﷺ. Both the sources inform us about the practical aspects of Divine commandments for human life and provide explanations and demonstrations of the basic principles outlined by Allah.

Ramadan is the month of blessings and without doubt a training course for a believer in which he/she is supposed to "loot the mercies" of Almighty Allah. The main purpose of Fasting is to restrain Nafs, so that a believer cherishes the love of Allah, which would ultimately land him in Allah's paradise. Our beloved Prophetﷺ said. 'The five (daily) Salah, and from one Jumu'ah prayer to the next Jumu'ah prayer, and from Ramadan to Ramadan are expiation for the (sins) committed in between (their intervals); provided the major sins aren't committed (Sahih Muslim).

It gives me immense pleasure to jot down few lines about the book, titled "As-Saum (Fasting): A Brief Introduction in the Light of Quran and Sahih Hadith" written by my dear brother and friend Dr. Fasil Barkat. He has explained the said topic efficiently in a simple style with full conviction. May Allah give more power to his pen, and may Allah increase his sincerity and bless him in every sphere of life. This book will prove beneficial to Muslims as well as to Non-Muslims, as for non-Muslims these efforts will surely make it easy for them to understand one of the fundamentals of Islam i.e. fasting, its essence and prosperity.

In concluding lines, I pray to Allah, may He accept this effort of my brother, and may He bestow His blessings on him in this world and hereafter, Ameen.

(Dr. Ismail Ibraheem)
Palpora, Noorbagh, Srinagar

Preface

Assalam-u-Alaykum!

All praise is due to Allah, the Lord of the worlds (Surat Al-Fateha, 1:2). May Allah's peace and blessings be upon His Final Prophet and Messenger, Muhammad ﷺ His ﷺ family and His ﷺ Companions.

Islam is the religion of peace and tranquility and at the same time the religion of utmost discipline and values. It instills and propagates the faith that outshines a believer in this world and the hereafter. Islam enlightens about every aspect of life and guides to lead a peaceful and healthy life. The complete guidance of Islam has left no scope for any doubts and confusions that could dominate with the negative perceptions in a believer's mind. While performing any religious onus, a believer often comes across questions and doubts demanding a believer to explore.

As-Saum (fasting) is one such compulsory Islamic duty about which every believer must have adequate knowledge in order to perform this important duty in a manner as desired by Allah and His Messenger ﷺ. The status of As-Saum (fasting) could very well be understood by the fact that it stands as one of the five pillars of Islam.

This humble effort of compilation on one of the main fundamentals of Islam is an honest effort to bring forth the niceties of "fasting". The aim is to apprise the reader about the real spirit behind this main pillar of Islam.

In the Holy Quran, Allah the Most Exalted Ordains:
"..... *Put your trust in Allah if you are believers indeed.*"
(Surat-ul-Maeeda5:23)
Thus, putting our trust whole-heartedly in Allah, we become the true and cherished believers and faithful. And with regard to fasting, Allah, the most Merciful and Benevolent in the Holy book states: -

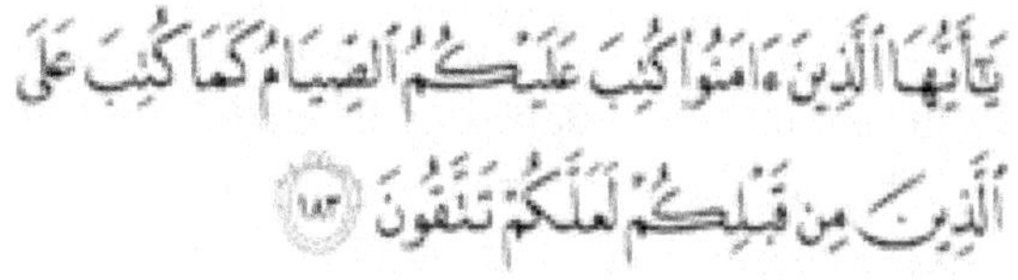

"O, you who believe! Observing the fasting is prescribed for you as it was prescribed for those before you, that you may become Al-Muttaqun (guard yourselves against evil)."
(Surat Al-Baqarah, 2:183)
In another verse Allah Ordains:

شَهْرُ رَمَضَانَ الَّذِى أُنزِلَ فِيهِ الْقُرْءَانُ هُدًى لِّلنَّاسِ وَبَيِّنَتٍ مِّنَ الْهُدَى وَالْفُرْقَانِ فَمَن شَهِدَ مِنكُمُ الشَّهْرَ فَلْيَصُمْهُ وَمَن كَانَ مَرِيضًا أَوْ عَلَى سَفَرٍ فَعِدَّةٌ مِّنْ أَيَّامٍ أُخَرَ يُرِيدُ اللَّهُ بِكُمُ الْيُسْرَ وَلَا يُرِيدُ بِكُمُ الْعُسْرَ وَلِتُكْمِلُوا الْعِدَّةَ وَلِتُكَبِّرُوا اللَّهَ عَلَى مَا هَدَىٰكُمْ وَلَعَلَّكُمْ تَشْكُرُونَ ۝

"*The month of Ramadan is the month when the Quran was sent down as guidance for mankind with clear proofs of guidance and the criterion by which to distinguish right from wrong. Therefore, whoever of you is present in that month, let him fast; but he who is ill or on a journey shall fast a similar number of days later on. Allah desires ease for you, not hardship. He desires you to fast the whole month, so that you may glorify Him for His having guided you and so that you may be grateful to Him.*"

(Surat Al-Baqarah, 2:185)

The above verses from the glorious Quran clearly reflect the importance of fasting and that of the month of Ramadan. It is the month in which the servants of Allah fast for His sake, which means they keep away from all the things/doings that are otherwise permissible in normal days.

Fasting is an act of seeking the pleasure of Allah by adhering to His orders. In the month of Ramadan Allah blesses His servants with opportunities to increase their Imaan (Faith) and reserve a magnificent place in Jannah.

There is an unending list of bounties that Allah promises for a believer who observes his Saum (fast) sincerely for Allah alone.

With this backdrop, this humble effort has been divided into seven well-drawn chapters covering the genesis of fasting along with permissible and non-permissible acts during fasting. This is followed by a description of things that invalidate fasting and making up for missed fasts. A full chapter has been devoted to Taraweeh prayers followed by Rewards of Fasting. The inspiration behind compiling this booklet is to understand the rudimentary elements of As-Saum(fasting). We have a lot of literature available but little time to invest in reading. Keeping in view all this, I have tried to explain (strictly in the light of Quran and Shahih Hadith)very briefly the elements of As-Saum,to be relished by the readersparticularly those avoiding thick books.

I have no words to thank and praise Allah for all his blessings. It is the mercy of Allah who favoured me and provided me the ability to compile this brief booklet about As-Saum.

Even though this is the fourth edition of this book and in every edition, I try to study and add some more information about As-Saum but keeping in view the vastness of this topic every edition is going to be a challenge in terms of collecting knowledge from authentic source alone.

Lastly, acknowledging the fact that being just a learner, there is every possibility for mistakes. I ask Allah to forgive my mistakes and shortcomings in this work and in general.

(Dr.Fasil Barkat)

Islamic University, J&K

March, 2022

Acknowledgements

I have no words to thank and praise Allah for all his blessings. It is the mercy of Allah who favoured me and provided me the ability to compile this brief booklet about As-Saum.

I am highly thankful to Prof. Khurshid Ali, my beloved uncle, mentor and guide for his valuable suggestions. Also, I am grateful to Dr. Sheikh Abdul Wahid (who has studied at The Islamic University of Madinah) for his remarkable recommendations. My sincere thanks to my beloved friend and brother Dr. Ismail Ibraheem for writing a foreword and encouraging me to compile this work.

I would like to thank my parents Mr. Barkat Ali, Mrs. Rafiqa Bano and sisters for their support and best wishes. I cannot forget to thank Allah for the folded tiny hand of my niece Neemat and nephews Nooraiz and Nawfal praying to Allah for my health and success.

I acknowledge and am sincerely indebted to my wife Dr. Mir Nouf Qayum, my children, Abdullah and Mahumfor their incessant moral support to compile this booklet for the sake of Allah.

(Dr.Fasil Barkat)

CHAPTER ONE

AS-SAUM

In Arabic terminology fast is known as As-Saum. It is observed from dawn to dusk and is an act of not drinking, eating and keeping away from acts that invalidate the fast. As mentioned in Sahih Al-Bukhari, Abu Hurairah[RA] narrates:

Allah'sMessenger[SAW]said, "Saum (fasting) is a shield (or a screen or a shelter from the Hell-fire). So, the person observing Saum should avoid sexual relation with his wife and should not behave foolishly and impudently, and if somebody fights with him or abuses him, he should say to him twice, 'I am observing Saum.' The Prophet[SAW]added, 'ByHim in Whose Hands my soul is, the smell coming out from the mouth of a person observing Saum is better with Allah then the smell of musk. (Allah says about the fasting person), 'He has left his food, drink and sexual desires for My Sake. The Saum (fast) is for Me i.e. Allah, so I will reward (the fasting person) for it and the reward of good deeds is multiplied ten times."

(Sahih Al-Bukhari volume 3, Chapter 2 Hadith No 1894)

Elements of As-Saum

As-Saum is compulsory upon ever adult believer. The month of Saum i.e. Ramadan comes with myriad benedictions relished by the Ummah of Prophet Muhammadﷺ.It is important to note that if any deed/act has countless bounties stored,it's obviously going to be a hard-hitting job involvingextreme hard work and patience. In other words,the treasure and pleasure hidden inside any deed needs to be earned in the very first case.

For being counted among the sincere slaves of Allah itdemandsfrom believersto have unquestionable and blind faith on Him, not only during the favorable times but at the times of mishaps and tragedies. It is in this context that we shall be discussing the niceties of As-Saum in the lines to follow.

Fasting is obligatory for a person if he/shefulfills the followingfive conditions:

1. He/She is a Muslim;
2. He/Sheis accountable (Mukallaf i.e. one who has reached the age of puberty and is of sound mind);
3. He/Sheis able to fast;
4. He/Sheis settled (not travelling); &
5. There are no impediments tohis/her fasting.

(Islamqa, 26814)

Being a Muslim means having faith that there is no god but Allah and Prophet Muhammadﷺis the messenger of Allah.

Secondly, a believer who shall be held amenablefor not observing Saum must have reached the age of puberty having a sound mind (i.e. is not insane).The signs of puberty are any of these: reaching the age of fifteen, nocturnal emissions (wet dreams), growth of coarse hairs around the private parts and additionally in case of females there is a forth sigh, which is Menstruation. (Islamqa, 20475)

Thirdly, he/she must be able to fast without jeopardizinghis/herlife as in case having some kind of medical issue etc. Being unable to fast falls into two categories: temporary inability and permanent inability. Temporary inability is that which is mentioned in the verse Surat Al-Baqarah, 2:185, such as one who is sick but hopes to recover, and the traveler. These people are allowed not to fast, then they have to make up what they missed.

Those who are permanently unable to fast, such as one who is sick and has no hope of recovery, or those who are elderly and are unable to fast, are mentioned in the verse Surat Al-Baqarah, 2:184.

Fourthly, a traveller enjoys the concessionin respect that fasting is not obligatory for him/her as mentioned in the verse Surat Al-Baqarah, 2:185.

Finally, there should be no impediments, this applies specifically to women. Women who are menstruating or bleeding following childbirth should not fast, because the Prophet said: "It is not the case that whenshe gets her periods, she does not pray or fast?" She has to make up the days missed.

(Al-Sharh al-Mumti', 6/330)

When As-Saum is not obligatory

It is imperativeto note that As-Saum is obligatory and stands as one of the pillars of Islam, we must be aware of the fact that missing aSaum purposely credits a great amount of sin into the believers account; yet, at the same time we must note that Islam has notmade fasting obligatory in the following cases:-

i.   Any person who is chronically ill and fears that fasting might aggravate his/her illness.
v.   Any women who is pregnant and breast feeding her child.
v.   Any women in her menstruation or postnatal periods.
v.   Anyone who is insane, in coma, unconscious, or very old and weak.
v.   Any person who is a traveler and suffersfrom the length of journey.

(Al-Sharh al-Mumti, 6/330)

Expiation for missed As-Saum

Islam has kept provisions for all those who miss to fast during the month of Ramadan due to any of the above said reasons. Such persons have been asked to make-up for those missed days of Ramadan.Those who are physically incapable of fasting, such as the chronically or terminally ill, are permitted to break the fast. However, later they have to feed a poor person for every missed day. In other words, their expiation of feeding the needy is equal to observing the fast. In this regard the Holy Quran ordains:

أَيَّامًا مَّعْدُودَٰتٍ فَمَن كَانَ مِنكُم مَّرِيضًا أَوْ عَلَىٰ سَفَرٍ فَعِدَّةٌ مِّنْ أَيَّامٍ أُخَرَ وَعَلَى ٱلَّذِينَ يُطِيقُونَهُ فِدْيَةٌ طَعَامُ مِسْكِينٍ فَمَن تَطَوَّعَ خَيْرًا فَهُوَ خَيْرٌ لَّهُ وَأَن تَصُومُوا خَيْرٌ لَّكُمْ إِن كُنتُمْ تَعْلَمُونَ ١٨٤

"[Fasting for] a limited number of days. So whoever among you is ill or on a journey [during them]- then an equal number of days [are to be made up]. And upon those who are able [to fast, but with hardship]- a ransom [as substitute] of feeding a poor person [each day]. And whoever volunteer excess-it is better for him. But to fast is best for you, if you only knew."

(Surat Al-Baqarah, 2:184)

CHAPTER TWO

OBSERVING AS-SAUM

As-Saum stands on two pillars that are:

1. The intention and
2. Refraining from things that break the fast

However, in addition to the above pillars, As-Saum includes some other desirable doings that need to be taken care of. A brief description of various elements of As-Saum will be discussed hereunder as per the regulation laid down by Islam. In the first instance, there has to be an intention to fasting, followed by pre-dawn meals, abstaining from certain acts during the duration of the fast and finally breaking the fast. Adherence to the principles laid down by Islam about As-Saum is very important, a thoughtful mistake and casual approach need to be taken care of. The fact of the matter is that the month of Ramadan (month of fasting) demands extra care from a believer in respect of his loom towards Islam. Thus it is very important for a believer to always try and learn about every aspect of As-Saum.

The diagram given below shall make it easy to understand:

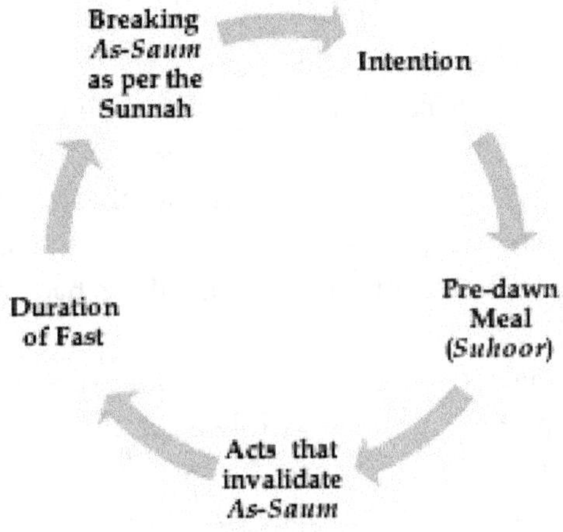

Intention:

A believer must know that all the deeds whether offering Salah, giving Zakaah or any good act depends on his intention. Unless the intention is to please Allah and is in accordance with the Sunnah (whatever is narrated from or about the Prophet Muhammadﷺ of words, actions or approval) of his Messengerﷺ no reward shall be expected. Thus, whenever we observe Saum it must be only to please Allah. Intentions are to be made in heart; no loud utterance is needed for Allah knows what dwells in our hearts. It is essential to make the intention to fast during the month of Ramadan at night, before the Fajr (dawn prayer). It is not sufficient to start fasting that day without the intentions. In case of the obligatory fast the intention must be made the night before the fast begins i.e. every believer must make his intention at night to observe his fast from early morning the next day.

Allah's Messengerﷺ said:

"Whoever does not determine to fast before the dawn, his fasting is null and void." (1)

However, with regard to Nafil(non-obligatory) fasts, it is permissible to make the intention to fast on the day we fast. If the believer has not eaten or drunk or had intercourse after Fajr his fast is valid.

Regarding such non-obligatory Saum, a Hadith narrated by Hazrat Aisha[RA] makes it vividly clear. It states:

The Prophetﷺentering home her one day at Duha (2) time and said, "Do you have anything (any food)?" She said, "No." He said, "Then I am fasting."

(Narrated by Muslim in his Saheeh, No. 1154)

Pre-dawn Meal:

As the word signifies it is the meal taken before the dawn. In Arabic pre-dawn meal is called Suhoor, which a believer has to take after his intention for the fast. Some people take the pre-dawn meal casual, Allah's Messengerﷺsaid:

"The difference between our fasting and that of the People of the Scriptures is the Suhoor (Pre-dawn meal)." (Sahi Ibn Hiban, No. 2377)

In another Hadith, Allah's Messengerﷺ said:

"Taking the pre-dawn meal in Ramadan is a blessing, so do not leave it, even it is drinking a mouthful of water. Allah, the Noble and the Might, and His angels send blessings over those who have taken the pre-dawn meal." (3)

Acts that Invalidate As-Saum:

There are certain things, if those are committed by a person keeping fast, the same invalidates this Saum. A detailed description of the same has been dealt with separately in the chapter titled, "Doings that invalidate As-Saum".

Duration of As-Saum:

The duration of a Saum is from the dawn to sunset. Before the dawn (Fajr), a believer has to take his pre-dawn meal (Suhoor) and abstain from everything that invalidates the fast until sunset.

Breaking As-Saum as per the Sunnah:

Breaking the Saum without any delay is the Sunnah of Allah's Messengerﷺ. A believer must break his fast immediately after the sunset without any further delay. Such an act is called as hastening to break the fast. People who hesitate to break the fast even after sunset and wait till dusk or until deep nightfall's must know that this was the practice of Jews and Christians during the era of Allah's Messengerﷺ. As such Allah's Messengerﷺ commanded every believer to contradict the Jews and Christians and hasten to break the fast immediately after the sunset. Allah's Messengerﷺ said:

"*People will continue to adhere to good as long as they hasten to break the fast.*"

(*Al-Bukhari, No. 1957 and Muslim, No. 1098*)

Breaking fast must be as per the practice of our beloved Prophet Muhammadﷺ. However, it is very sad we rather prefer to do it as per our own desires and practices. Allah's Messengerﷺ used to break his fast with three fresh dates. In the non-availability of fresh dates, Heﷺ would eat three dry dates; and if there were no dry dates even, Heﷺ would take three sips of water." (4)

While breaking the fast, the Holy Prophetﷺ, would supplicate as follows: (5)

"Dhahabaz-zamauwabtallatil- uruqu, wathabatalajru, in shaa Allah."

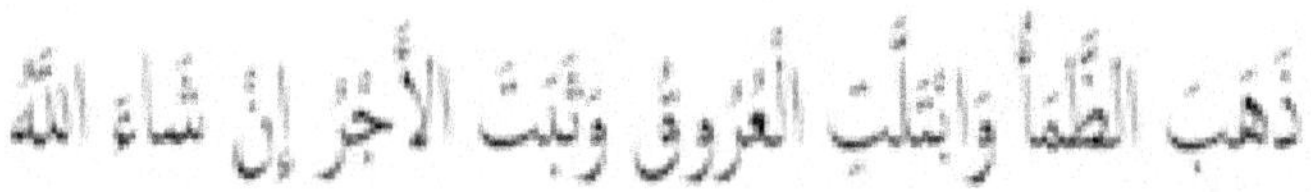

(The thirst is gone, and the veins replenished, and the reward is confirmed, if Allah wills)

CHAPTER THREE

PERMISSIBLE DOINGS DURING AS-SAUM

Acts that, if committed, will not affect the Saum, whatsoever. The details of the same are as follows:

- Any believer who has to observe fast but is in the state of impurity can have pre-dawn meal and observer his Saum however; he must take a full bath to offer his prayer.

Narrated Aa'ishah[RA] and Umm Salama[RA]:
"At times Allah's Messenger used to get up in the morning in the state of Janaba (sexual impurity) after having sexual relations with his wives. He would then take a bath and observe Saum (fast)."
(*Al-Bukhari Vol 3 Chapter 22 Hadith No. 1925,26*)

- It is allowed to kiss and embrace one's wife while fasting. Aa'ishah[RA] narrates:

"Allah's Messenger ﷺ used to kiss and embrace (his wives) while he was observing Saum (fast), and he had more power to control his desire than any of you."

(Al-Bukhari Vol 3 Chapter 23 Hadith No. 1927)

The above Hadith clarifies that fondling and kissing one's wife is permissible even if one is fasting however, the same is exclusively limited to those who have self-control. Contemporary scholars hold the firm views that if the fasting person is young, then the same must be avoided and those who are older such acts are acceptable.

- It is permissible to go for medicinal injections for a fasting person as far these injections are not food or any kind of nourishments. (Standing Committee for Academic Research And Issuing Fatwas, 10/252).
- Removal of teeth is also permissible [Shaykh Ibn Baaz (may Allah have mercy on him) 15/285].
- It is permissible to cool oneself with water during fasting (Al-Bukhari, Vol. 3 Chapter 25).
- Cupping to drain blood is permissible while fasting, as narrated Ibn Abbas [RA]

"The Prophet ﷺ has cupped while he was in a state of Ihram, and also he was observing a Saum (fast)." (Al-Bukhari, Chapter 32 Hadith No. 1938). Cupping of blood is the process of drawing blood to the surface of the skin by creating a vacuum at that point.

- It is permissible to put medication in eye or ear even though they find their way to throat. (Al-Sharh al-Mumti', 6/382)
- It is permissible to clean our mouths using the Miswak (tooth stick) [Al-Bukhari, Vol.3 Chapter 25].

- It is permissible to taste the food out from the pot.(Al-Bukhari, Vol. 3 Chapter 25). However, the food must not enter inside, nor it must be swallowed and here the scholars are of the opinion that it must be done only at the time of extreme necessity.
- Most of the scholars (including Sheikh Bin Baaz[RA]) are of the opinion that using toothpaste is permissible however, the same must not be swallowed.(Majmoo Fataawa al-Shaykh Ibn Baaz 15/260)
- If a person vomits unintentionally it doesn't break the fast, as narrated by (Al Trimidhi Hadith No. 720 Book of Fasting/Sunan Abu Dawud Vol.2 Book of fasting Hadith no. 2374)
- Using aerosol to remove bad breath in Ramadan if nothing from it reaches the throat. However, it is enough to use the siwaak which the Prophet ﷺ encouraged us to use. Besides this breath is not something to be disliked, because in the Hadith it says that, "The smell from the fasting person's mouth is better in the sight of Allah than the fragrance of musk."
  - *(Al-Bukhari, No. 1904 and Muslim, No. 1151)*

CHAPTER FOUR

DOINGS THAT INVALIDATE AS-SAUM

Below given is the description of acts that invalidate Saum: -

- Sexual intercourse (while a believer is observing Saum) with wife turns the Saum (fast) null and void. As a consequence of this, a person has to make up for the day later besides paying the expiation for the same. This compensation to either to manumit a slave or observing Saum (fast) for two (02) months consecutively or feeding sixty (60) poor persons.

(Al-Bukhari Vol. 3 Chapter 30 Hadith No. 1936)

- Vomiting intentionally breaks the fast (Al Trimidhi Hadith No. 720 Book of Fasting/Sunan Abu Dawud Vol.2 Book of fasting Hadith no. 2374).
- Deliberate eating or drinking invalidates the fast however, if anyone eats or drinks forgetfully or is forced

to do so, his fast is valid. In this regard the saying of the Holy Prophet ﷺ has been narrated by Hazrat Abu Hurairah[RA] as follows:

The Prophet ﷺ said, "if somebody eats or drinks forgetfully then he should complete his Saum (fast), for what he has eaten or drank, has been given to him by Allah."
(Al-Bukhari Vol 3 Chapter 26 Hadith No. 1933)

- Menstruation invalidates the fast. However, the concerned lady has to make up the missed Saum (fast) but not her missed Salah (prayer).

    (Al-Bukhari Vol 3 Chapter 41 Hadith No. 1950)

- Intentional ejaculation of the semen invalidates ones fast (Saum). However, unintentional ejaculation by way of a wet dream does not invalidate the fast (Islamqa, 38023).
- Transfusion of blood does invalidate the Saum (fast) as the same is a sort of nourishment. However, the mere loss of blood doesn't break the fast.

    (Shaykh Ibn Uthaymeen, Majaalis Shahr, Islamqa, 250660).

- Postpartum bleeding i.e. bleeding after childbirth.

In addition to the above there are many acts that a person observing Saum must desist from. These acts if doesn't break or invalidate the Saum but certainly reduce the reward. Among many such doings one is telling lies. In this context, as narrated by Hazrat Abu Hurairah[RA]:

The Prophet[saw] said, "Whoever does not give up lying speech (false statements) and acting on those lies and evil actions etc., Allah is not in need of his leaving his food and drink i.e. Allah will not accept his Saum (fast)."

(Al-Bukhari Vol 3 Chapter 8 Hadith No. 1903)

Making up for the missed As-Saum

One who misses the Saum because of travelling, illness, menstruation and post-childbirth bleedings must hasten to make up for Saum (fast) after Ramadan. Thus, one has to make up the same number of days of fasting, as he/she has missed on account of the above states reasons. In this regard the Holy Quran Ordains in Chapter 2:

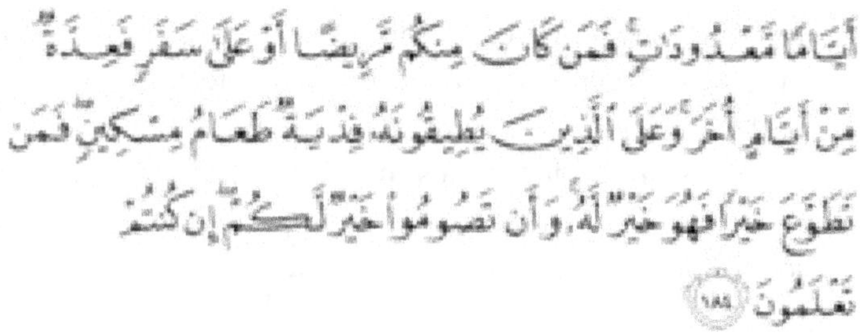

"[Fasting for] a limited number of days. So whoever among you is ill or on a journey [during them]- then an equal number of days [are to be made up]. And upon those who are able [to fast, but with hardship]- a ransom [as substitute] of feeding a poor person [each day]. And whoever volunteer excess-it is better for him. But to fast is best for you, if you only knew."

(Surat Al-Baqarah, 2:184)

Further, in case of a person who made a swearing to fast but missed the same in his lifetime it is his heirs to fulfill that. In this regard as narrated by Hazrat Ibn Abbas[RA]:

A man came to the Holy Prophetﷺ and said, "O Allah's Messenger! My mother died and she ought to have observed Saum (fast) one month (for her missed Ramadan). Shall I observe, Saum on her behalf?" The Prophetﷺ replied in the affirmative and said. 'Allah's debts have more right to be paid."

(Al-Bukhari Vol 3 Chapter 42 Hadith No. 1953)

TARAWEEH PRAYER

Taraweeh is the prayer which was known as the 'Night Prayer' (Qiyam-ul-Lail or Tahajjud) during the days of our beloved Prophet Muhammadﷺ and his Companions. The time to offer this Salah (prayer) is from Isha Sala until the Salah of Fajr. Narrated by Hazrat Abu Hurairah[RA]:

I heard Allah's Messengerﷺ saying regarding Ramadan, "Whoever performed Salah (prayer) at night in it (the month of Ramadan) with sincere faith and hoping for a reward from Allah, then all his past sins will be forgiven."

(Al-Bukhari Vol 3 Chapter 1 Hadith No. 2008)

The above Hadith clarifies the importance of the night prayer in the month of Ramadan. We have to clear one thing that it was not only the month of Ramadan when our beloved Prophet Muhammadﷺ used to pray the night prayer rather Heﷺ used to pray the night prayer throughout the year.

One of the sensitive discussions during the month Ramadan is all about the number of Rak'ahs in Taraweeh prayer. This is something we pay no heed to during the rest of year, as if this prayer (Taraweeh) is specific for Ramadan only. A Muslim is the brother of his fellow Muslim and it's a matter of concern that we get divided on issues wherein a difference of opinions is acceptable. We must be aware of the fact that differences existed between Sahaabah's (Prophet'sﷺ Companions) also, yet their hearts remained united. In this context, Shaykh Ibn Uthaymeen (may Allah have mercy on him) aptly explains:

"It is not right to go to the extremes or becoming negligent. As some hop to the extremes in adhering to the number of Rak'ahs mentioned in the Sunnah and say that it is not possible to do more than the number mentioned in the Sunnah, and aggressively denounce those who do more than that, saying that they are sinners which as per the opinion of Shaykh is undoubtedly wrong".

(Islamqa, 9036)

Prophetﷺ upon being asked about the night prayers, said, "that they are to be done two by two", and Heﷺ didn't specify any particular number. The evidence that there is no set number for prayers at night including Taraaweeh prayer is the Hadith of Ibn 'Umer[RA] according to which a man asked the Prophet Muhammadﷺ about prayer at night. The Prophetﷺ said, "prayer at night are to be offered two by two (two Rak'ahs at a time). If any of you fears that the time of sawn is approaching, then let him pray one Rak'ah as Witr."

(Al-Bukhari, 846; Muslim, 749)

Of course, the one who asked about the night prayer did not know the number, because if he did not know how to do it, it is even more likely that he did not know the number. And he was not one of those who served the Prophetﷺ so that we might say that he knew what happened inside his house. Since the Prophetﷺ told him how to do it but did not say how many times, it may be understood that the matter is broader in scope, and that a person may pray one hundred Rak'ahs then pray Witr with one Rak'ah.

In another Hadith narrated by Hazrat Aa'ishah[RA] mentioned in Sahih Al Bukhari and Sahih Muslim that Prophet Muhammad never exceeded Eleven (11) Rak'ah in Ramadan or any other month (eight Rak'ah and three as Witr prayer]

(Al-Bukhari Vol 2 Chapter 16 Hadith No. 1147)

The point is that one who prays eleven Rak'ahs in the manner narrated from the Prophet is doing well and is following the Sunnah. Whoever makes the recitation shorter and increases the number of Rak'ahs is also doing well. A person who does either of these two things is not to be denounced.

Shaykh al-Islam Ibn Taymiyah (may Allah have mercy on him) is of the opinion:

"If a person prays Taraaweeh according to the madhhabs of Abu Haneefa, al-Shaafa'i and Ahmad, with twenty Rak'ahs, or according to the madhhab of Maalik, with thirty-six Rak'ahs, or with thirteen or eleven Rak'ahs he has done well, as Imam Ahmad said, because there is nothing to specify the number. So, the greater or lesser number of Rak'ahs depends on how long or short the qiyaam (standing in the prayer) is".

(Al-Ikhtiyaaraat, p. 64)

Further, regarding the subject of offering Taraweeh prayer in Masjid or home, there is a clear Hadith that beloved Prophet Muhammad offered the night prayer in the middle of the night in the month of Ramadan for three days in Masjid. Afterwards Prophet Muhammad prayed at home.

(Al-Bukhari Vol 3 Chapter 1 Hadith No. 2012)

After the Prophet Muhammadﷺ left this world, people continued to offer Night Prayers individually, and not in congregation. The process remained same during the Caliphate of Hazrat Abu Bakr[RA] and in the early days of Caliphate Hazrat Umar[RA]. Subsequently, Hazrat Umar[RA] deemed it proper to ask for offering Taraweeh in Masjid in congregation. The genesis of the same have been made clear by Ibn Shihab: Abdur Rahman bin Abdul Qari, who narrates as follows:

"I went out in the company of Umer bin Al-Khattab[RA] one night in Ramadan to the mosque and found the people performing Salah (prayers) in different groups. A man performing Salah (prayers) alone, or a man performing Salah (prayers) with a little group behind him. So Umer[RA] said, 'In my opinion I would better collect these (people) under the leadership of one Qari (reciter) [i.e. let them perform Salah (prayers) in congregation]. So, he made up his mind and he congregated them behind Ubai bin Kab. Then on another night I went again in his company and the people were performing Salah (prayers) behind their reciter. On that, Umer[RA] remarked, 'What an excellent Bidah (i.e. innovation in religion) this is; but the Salah (prayers) which they do not perform, and sleep at its time is superior than the one they are performing now.' He meant the Salah (prayers) in the last part of the night. (In those days) people used to perform Salah (prayers) in the early part of the night."

(Al-Bukhari Vol 3 Chapter 1 Hadith No. 2010)

Let us not get confused by the word innovation (Bidah) used by Hazrat Umer bin Al-Khattab[RA] so as what he meant by calling it an innovation was in the linguistic sense, i.e., it was something new that people had never done before. Shaykh al-Islam Ibn Taymiyah (may Allah have mercy on him) referring to it said:

This is a description in linguistic terms, not in a technical shar'i sense. That is because the word innovation (Bidah) in linguistic terms includes everything that is introduced without precedent. If the words of Allah's Messengerﷺ indicate that something is recommended or obligatory after his death, or is indicated in general terms, even though it was not done until after his death such as the book of charity (a document that listed the rates of Zakaah on livestock) that Abu Bakr[RA] issued then doing that action after his death may correctly be called an innovation in linguistic terms, because it was something new. Also, any such deed which is supported by the Quran and Sunnah is not an innovation in shar'i terms, even if it may be described as an innovation is more general in meaning in the linguistic sense than in the technical shar'i sense.

(Iqtida' as-Siraat al-Mustaqeem 2/95-97)

CHAPTER SIX

THE BLESSED NIGHTS OF RAMADAN

Among the countless blessings a Muslim enjoys in the blessed month of Ramadan are the blessed nights. Every night of Ramadan is a blessing but the odd nights commencing from the 21st of Ramadan till its end holds special place on account of many reasons. Allah the mighty enlightens in Chapter 97:

إِنَّا أَنْزَلْنَاهُ فِي لَيْلَةِ الْقَدْرِ ۞ وَمَا أَدْرَاكَ مَا لَيْلَةُ الْقَدْرِ ۞ لَيْلَةُ الْقَدْرِ خَيْرٌ مِنْ أَلْفِ شَهْرٍ ۞ تَنَزَّلُ الْمَلَائِكَةُ وَالرُّوحُ فِيهَا بِإِذْنِ رَبِّهِمْ مِنْ كُلِّ أَمْرٍ ۞ سَلَامٌ هِيَ حَتَّى مَطْلَعِ الْفَجْرِ ۞

In this Chapter Allah the mighty informs about some events that are associated with one special Night called *Al-*

Qadr. It is the Night when Al-Quran was sent and it is this Night which is better than a thousand months. There are numerous *Hadiths* that explain the importance and uniqueness of the night of *Al-Qadr.* Imam Ahmad recorded that Abu Hurayarah[RA] said, "When Ramadan would come, the Messenger of Allah would say:

Verily, the month of Ramadan has come to you all. It is a blessed month, which Allah has obligated you all to fast. During it the gates of Paradise are opened, the gates of Hell are closed and the devils are shackled. In it there is a Night that is better than one thousand months. Whoever is deprived of its good, then he has truly deprived.

(Ahmad 2: 230)

In another Hadith narrated by Aby Hurayrah[RA] the Messenger of Allah said:

Whoever stands (in prayer) during the Night of Al-Qadr with faith and expecting reward (from Allah), he will be forgiven for his previous sins.

(Fath Al Bari 4: 294, and Muslim 1:523)

Keeping this in mind a beleiver must make it sure to find this blessed night among the last five odd nights of the blessed month of Ramadan.

CHAPTER SEVEN

RAMADAN REWARDS

Allah has promised a great reward to those who fast because the virtue of fasting is so great. In fact, Allah has not specified the reward for it, rather as per a Hadith Qudsi, He ordains:

"...except for fasting, for it is for Me, and I shall reward for it."

(Al-Bukhari, 5927: Muslim, 1151)

Again Allah has promised all those who fast to make them enter the paradise through the gate meant just for them. In this regard, as narrated by Sahl[RA]:

"The Prophet said. "There is a gate in Paradise called Al-Rayyaan, and those who observe Saum (fasts) will enter through it on the Day of Resurrection and none except them will enter through it. It will be said. 'Where are those who used to observe Saum (fast)? They will get up and none except them will enter through it. After their entry the gate will be closed, and nobody will enter through it."

(Al-Bukhari, 1763: Muslim, 1947)

Further, the month of Ramadan is blessed with a night, regarding which the Holy Quran proclaims:

إِنَّا أَنْزَلْنَاهُ فِي لَيْلَةِ الْقَدْرِ - وَمَا أَدْرَاكَ مَا لَيْلَةُ الْقَدْرِ - لَيْلَةُ الْقَدْرِ

خَيْرٌ مِنْ أَلْفِ شَهْرٍ

"Indeed, We sent the Qurán down during the Night of Decree. And what can make you know what is the Night of Decree? The Night of Decree is better than a thousand months."

(Surat-ul-Qadar, 97:1-3)

Zakaat al-Fitr is another reward a believer has been blessed with. In this regard Hazrat Ibn 'Abbaas[RA] narrates:

The Messenger of Allah[ﷺ] enjoined Zakaat al-Fitr as a purification for the fasting person from idle and obscene speech, and to feed the poor. Whoever gives it before the prayer, it is Zakaat al-Fitr, and whoever gives it after the prayer, it is ordinary charity. (6)

Conclusion

Blessed are the persons who observe Saum (fast) in the month of Ramadan, as per the instructions of Allah, and the Sunnah of His Prophet Muhammadﷺ.

Let us not brawl and maledict each other, rather let us pledge to put our sincere efforts and beg Allah for Magfirah (forgiveness).The blessed month of Ramadan multiplies the reward for our good deeds. The motto of observing As-Saum, performing Taraweeh and other deeds should be to attain the pleasure Allah. Let us restrain and keep ourselves away from marathons, wherein The Noble Quran is recited or made to recite in haste. We must always pray Allah with sincerity and faith, let us not get divided by submitting to the whispers of Iblees.

Let us conclude with the supplication that, May Allah protect and bless us with His choicest blessings. May all our deeds be accepted by Allah and the month of Ramadan brings felicity in our lives. May Allah help us to learn and imbibe what is right and acceptable to Him. May peace and blessings be upon our beloved Prophet Muhammadﷺ, Hisﷻ family and Hisﷻ Companions, Ameen.

Dr. Fasil Barkat
drfaisalbarkat@gmail.com
faisal.barkat@islamicuniversity.edu.in

vvvvvvvvv

References

1. Ahmad and the four Sunan Compliers graded authentic by Shaikh Al-Albani in Sahih Al-Jami' As-Saghir, No.6539.
2. Ishraaq prayer is Duha, it is called Ishraaq because is done immediately after sunrise
3. Ahmad, graded authentic by Shaikh Al-Albani in Sahih Al-Jami' As-Saghir, No.3683.
4. AbuDawud and others, graded authentic by Shaikh Al-Albani in Sahih Al-Jami' As-Saghir, No.4995.
5. This Hadith is authentic recorded by Abu Dawud and others graded Hasan by Shaikh Al-Albani in Al-Irwaa'Al-Ghaleel, No.920.
6. Abu Dawood and classed as Hasan by al-Albaani in Saheeh Abi Dawood.

www.ingramcontent.com/pod-product-compliance
Lightning Source LLC
Chambersburg PA
CBHW060921130726

48001CB00006B/2353